Finding your Soulmate after 40: The Smart Woman's Guide

By Elizabeth Ward

Copyright

Dedication

We've been through so much together
You were born my sister
You have become my heart friend
I am so grateful that you were born
and that I get to walk this path with you
I hope this book will make you proud to be its inspiration.
My sister, my soulmate, my heart friend.
I love you Ems

Table of Contents

Elizabeth Ward

It's Never too Late to Find your Soulmate

We recognize a soulmate by the supreme level of comfort and security we feel with that person. That doesn't mean that there aren't issues that remain to be ironed out. Rather, it means we know intuitively that we can resolve issues with our soul mate without losing his or her love and respect.
~Linda Brady

Gemma returned from a glorious weekend spa retreat with her best friend, refreshed, rejuvenated, and in that painstakingly honest place that self-care creates where you can no longer hide from the true longings of your heart. She came to me and admitted that while she loves her work and is generally happy and content in her life, what she really wants is to get married and have her own little family. She is 43 years old, has never been married, and is a key leader at a respected corporation. She has had 2 serious love relationships, her first one in her early 20's; it was her first love and it ended when he moved away and went to college. After she graduated college, she jumped into work and worked her way up the corporate ladder, sometimes putting in 90-hour work weeks, often getting home at 10pm at night or later. Now in her 40's, long work days and working on weekends has become the norm, she manages a team, has grown as a leader and makes a 6-figure income. Through the years, as time permitted, she had a few hook ups and short dating relationships, but none that ever made her feel like "happily ever after." She got close in her mid 30's when she had a short-lived, yet very passionate relationship where she fell hard for him, and thought his feelings were reciprocal, but when he broke it off with her, and then got engaged to another woman just 3 months later, a piece of her closed up inside.

For the past several years she has been in a casual relationship with a man and they are essentially "f*ck buddies." While she enjoys the sex with him, and he makes her feel wanted and sexy, there is no depth of connection beyond the sex and many of his habits even annoy her. Whenever she tries to fit him into the mold of "soulmate" and her "happily ever after" man, the compatibility issues between them just don't work. They don't live together and only see each other for their weekend getaways as their schedules permit. For now it is working for her...kinda. Except when she gets some time to really reflect and look at her life and then this longing bubbles up from deep inside of her and comes to the surface once again. What if there is more...what if I am missing out on something even better and settling? Because what she really wants is a soulmate relationship and to be married with a family. She wants to have a partner in her life who can be by her side through all of the ups and downs, a companion to ease the load of responsibility off of her shoulders and to go to events, family get togethers, walks with her dog and travel to delightful places with her.

She has a large family and a huge group of friends and acquaintances that she spends her free time with on the evenings and weekends when she is not working. She has been at the grind of her job for so long now...it has just become normal to overwork, bang it out, get shit done, cross things off of her list. She thrives on projects, tasks and to-do lists, and is very comfortable and successful in her job and in her life. It's just this one little thing that she hasn't been successful at...yet.

Because of her high up position in her company, she is able to keep a reasonable work/life balance now compared to her younger years. She has achieved many of the financial, security, and career goals that she wanted for herself. And now...in her 40's, she wonders if there is more...she wants more...she wants it all...she wants the dream come true love and the happily ever after, she just hasn't yet figured out how to get it...how to have it all. So year after year, she stays in her comfort zone of work...at least here she knows what she is doing, at least in work she feels comfortable, competent and complete.

I understand Gemma's story because even though I didn't follow her exact career path, in many ways I was experiencing her frustration at not knowing how to achieve this soulmate relationship that I was longing for too. I know because I was alone for 7 years before I attracted my first soulmate. And I remember the questioning from couples and well-meaning family members...like I had to defend myself for being single...and of course the underlying implication that came through was...what was wrong with me? As if being "coupled" was the ultimate cure all for every ailment.

I remember burying myself in other activities where I felt "successful", all of the lonely nights and the times that I got stuck at the kids table just because I was single. I remember the questioning inside myself when people would ask why you are still single? And I would think...what's wrong with me? Other people can do this easily, why can't I?

I used to look at other women in relationships and wonder what they had that I didn't. I remember this deep longing in my heart to give love and connect in this depth of a relationship that would call out to me again and again. And I felt like I was trying everything that I knew to do...but nothing seemed to work.

I know you are afraid that time is running out and that maybe this just wasn't in the cards for you in this lifetime. I know it has been easier to bury yourself in your career, your personal growth, or your family's drama and that you've been very successful in many of your endeavors in life. I know that you are nailing it and every other area of your life except this one. And I know the secret question that keeps you up at night, because it kept me up too...What if there is something wrong with me?

I know how tired you are from all the questions about why you are still single. I know about all the advice you get from well-intended loved ones who can't possibly understand what it is like for you since they have never been through this themselves, perhaps having achieved a great relationship early on and marriage at an early age.

I know that a small part of you worries you are too old, not pretty enough, need to lose 20 lb, don't have enough time, have too many wrinkles, or some flaw that makes you unattractive or unlovable. I understand that your past relationships may have hurt your heart so bad, you wonder if you are even capable of opening your heart and loving again.

I know that you are kicking ass in so many other areas of your life and that for the most part you are happy and content in your life...exactly as it is. I was too. But every now and again...you get that longing in your heart that won't go away...no matter how much you work, spend time with friends or family or otherwise fill up your life. That longing that says...I know there is something more, something deeper...something special...and it is for me...I have always known it is for me...if only I knew how to get there from here.

My Soulmate Journey

*The place you are right now...God circled
on a map for you.*
~Hafiz

*I*n high school, I was never one of those girls that continually had a boyfriend, you know who I mean...those cute cheerleader types who either had a series of boyfriends or the ones who dated their high school sweetheart all throughout the high school years...I felt excluded from that club. It was the 80's and I was wearing leather jackets and heavy metal t-shirts, I smoked cigarettes and the crowd I hung out with were called "burnouts." Not to mention the fact that I had sprung up during 8th grade and was now a head taller than most of the boys my own age. I had some guys who seemed to like me enough to want to fool around with me, but I never had a steady "boyfriend" during my high school years. So, because of that, I made some conclusions about love and my lovability. I assumed that I was too tall, too strong willed, not pretty enough, too harsh, didn't have long enough hair, etc...that somehow this wasn't happening for me because I was flawed. If I could just be perfect enough, then surely someone would love me in that special way forever. Right?!

When I had my very first "love" relationship at 18...it was with an "older" man. He was 21 and he seemed so "worldly" and confident. I was just so...wounded (from years of perceived rejection) and desperate, quite frankly for someone to love me and prove that I was worthy of being loved. I needed evidence that I was loveable, and he seemed to provide it...at least in a way that was familiar to me...through rejection, criticism, and abuse. It was a tumultuous, intense 3-year relationship, I pursued him way too much in my attempt to get him to love me, and he was withholding towards me. And since neither of us knew what the hell we were doing, we easily fell into drama, fighting, and just acting in shitty ways towards each other in our ignorance about relationships. Thank God he broke up with me...I was devastated of course...it felt like my heart had been ripped out of my chest. You see I believed he was my soulmate...and looking back now, I know he was...he was my soulmate for a reason, to teach me to respect myself and not settle for shitty behavior or settle for "going for his potential" and not looking at the fact that who he was in that moment was way less than what I wanted. It was one of the most painful lessons of my life....one that could only be delivered from a "reason" soulmate.

I don't remember where I heard this...but it resonated so much that it has stuck with me through the years. Soulmates come into our life for a **reason**, a **season**, or a **lifetime**. Lemme explain. A "reason" soulmate comes into our life for a few months to a few years, during which time one major area in each soulmate's life is brought to light, supported and healed. How long it lasts depends on how quickly the lessons of that relationship are learned and integrated. Like learning how to stand up for yourself, a career change, or reaching an important goal. Reason soulmates, like any other soulmate relationship can be painful, passionate, productive and highly promising and then suddenly fizzle out for no apparent reason. This is because with "reason" soulmates there is a high degree of connection and chemistry but not enough compatibility for a long-term relationship.

What is frustrating is that the connection, chemistry, and commitment are very real and very strong, and the love is absolutely there...but then every time you try to fit them into the mold of a "season" or "forever" soulmate, it just doesn't work...it's like trying to fit a square peg in a round hole. And the longer you stay in the relationship, the more painful it gets, because once the lesson is finished, the soulmate mojo turns into its opposite, and what was once medicine and growth has now become stagnant, addictive and even toxic. What was once loved, now grates on the nerves, what was once no big deal, suddenly, feels intolerable. Once you have completed your mission together, learned the lesson or achieved the goal and fulfilled the purpose of the "reason" relationship, it is time to move on, as staying only delays both of your development.

A "season" soulmate is a long-term relationship from a few years to many years in which major childhood themes and wounding patterns can be uncovered, resolved and healed over the course of the relationship. A "season" soulmate can feel similar to a "lifetime" soulmate...all the way up until the end...when you realize that your focus has only been on healing the two of you within the relationship and when that is complete you have nowhere else to go together and your long time together comes to a close. This can be an incredibly painful experience when you are asked to reconcile the expectations of the relationship (we were supposed to be together forever) with the reality of it (this is a "season" soulmate relationship, we have done everything we could, we are no longer growing together and it is time to move on).

A "lifetime" soulmate relationship either starts out or evolves into serving the higher good of a larger, more global goal. Its sole purpose is to lift up humanity in some way. The relationship can be one of raising a stable, loving family, or combining careers to bring breakthrough information, technology, or healing to the world to make it a better place. And like the name implies, a "lifetime" soulmate lasts for a lifetime. And here's the rub...you only get to know which one they are when you reach the end of the relationship.

But I digress...back to my story. I was pretty wounded from that first soulmate relationship and after another failed relationship with a very sweet guy, I decided to take 7 years off from dating or being in a relationship. I was 23 years old and I obviously wasn't "getting it", so I decided to use that time to learn all I could about relationships (since I felt so ignorant in this area), and I started reading everything I could get my hands on about spiritual growth and how to heal my painful past and love myself in the process. At some point in that 7-year journey, I don't remember when, I learned about soulmates...

And from the minute I heard the term 'soulmates', I was hooked! I thought yes, that is for me...the answer to my problems of why I hadn't yet been successful in relationships...he would be my perfect partner, my missing half...the other side of my soul....the yin to my yang...we would understand each other without having to speak, blah, blah, blah...needless to say I was ridiculously romantic about it as only a 20-something can be. As I grew more intrigued with this topic, I decided to learn more about how to go about attracting one of these magical creatures into my own life. Looking back now, I believe I thought that if I was just a good enough person or did all the "right" things he would just magically appear at my door and sweep me off my feet as my reward for a job well done (well of course...right!?).

During this 7-year period, as I learned to listen to myself through meditation, love myself, heal my past and grow, I had a strong urging from within to move 3000 miles away to San

Diego, uprooting my solid Chicago upbringing, because my heart was whispering for me to do so. So, with only $300 to my name, my car loaded with all of my worldly possessions...I set off to make a life in San Diego. During my early time in San Diego, in my quest to bring a soulmate into my life, I remember sprinkling glitter around my front door (one books suggestion), going to the ocean to cast my wishes into the water (another book said this was how to attract him). I watched *Romeo and Juliet* (the one with Claire Danes and Leo DeCaprio) and cried my eyes out every time...my tears paying homage to my longing for him, for us, and all of that unrequited love that I had inside of me. I even made a soulmate box just for "him" with cards, poetry, love songs, pictures and gemstones (for our wedding rings of course).

It was the winter of 2000-2001, I had been in San Diego for a year, but I remember that winter was when I got "the call" the whisper that is was time for me to date again. Even though I had been avidly thinking/dreaming about "him" for years...something was different this winter because the whisper... it came from such a deep, quiet, calm part of myself...it just felt so...right.

In 2001 online dating hadn't taken off quite yet. I think people were just doing personal adds in the newspaper or going to bars in order to meet people back then...but that didn't feel right to me. So, not knowing what else to do, I just kinda prayed and opened up to the Universe and said that I was ready to date.

Shortly thereafter, I got set up on a blind date in the Spring, then I had a guy ask me out at work and had 1 (meh) date with him, then I dated a co-worker for about 2-3 months. During that time, we (the co-worker I was dating at the time) went and saw a movie...I think it was *Moulin Rouge*...but I remember there was a deep and intense love story in the movie and after seeing that movie with him, my heart just...ached. Because I knew that the guy I was currently dating wasn't my soulmate and our relationship would never reach that deep level that I was longing for. That night after the movie, I went home and I was so heart broken and pissed off at the Universe, God, and my years of bad luck at finding my soulmate that I wrote a 2 page "list" as a way to flip the bird to God, the Universe...all of it...I was just sick and tired of not having this great love in my life. I poured my heart out in this list and put everything I had ever wanted in a guy including the fact that he was my soulmate and our soul connection was deep and this was the stuff of fairy tales and dreams come true (once a romantic, always a romantic). I covered a single notebook page, front and back and even filled in the margins...it was packed!

After I wrote it I felt like, Ha!....take that God...let's see what you do with this mother-f*&!#r! Like I said, I was pretty pissed off and frustrated at this point. I wrote the list in June 2001 and my soulmate showed up in my life 8 weeks later in August 2001. It had worked...holy sh*t! I had somehow stumbled upon the answer to how to attract a soulmate. Happy dance....

What is ironic is that he had been under my nose for a year...we worked together and I hadn't even really noticed him before. Then after I made my list, it seemed like all of a sudden, one day he walked into the stockroom and just sort of "glowed".

He had been working on himself too and had lost 50 lbs over the past year and suddenly I just "saw" him. We were already working together but then started walking together and talking and hanging out and it all just felt so....'normal' and easy and right...like he was not only meant to be there with me...but he always had been. Our first kiss was good, but the second one was monumental...that combined with how it felt like heaven in his arms when he held me and how I could talk on the phone for hours with him was when I knew...this was something special.

I don't even remember when we said I love you...because it felt like I had always loved him...and he me...like it was as natural as breathing. Right from the start we were absolutely gaga about each other and stayed that way for a long time...people would often mistake us for a 'new' couple even after 5 years of being together.

In the early parts of our relationship, we were just so drunk on our love and our many shared commonalities that we would spend entire weekends holed up in my apartment, just basking in each other's love, it felt like time stood still in those moments we were together. We moved in together at a year and a half and went through many beautiful, life-changing and heartbreaking experiences together. We moved to Portland, hiked beautiful mountains, got married, changed jobs, earned degrees, shopped the farmers market every Sunday, dealt with addictions and finally cancer. He survived it, but our relationship did not.

We learned, grew, loved, healed, and changed in so many wonderful, positive ways throughout our journey together. We had a beautiful 10-year relationship together and I look back on that time with so much gratitude and overflowing love in my heart that I got to be a part of that magical journey during our 10 years together.

Remember...soulmates come into our life for a "reason", a "season", or a "lifetime". I had a beautiful "season" of 10 years with this soulmate. The form of our relationship changed, not the love. He will always be with me in a chamber of my heart as I know I am with him...always.

And then in 2011, I was back in Chicago again, surrounded by my family as I healed and went to school for my master's degree and rebuilt my life as a single person again. I was single for the next several years until I once again got the "call" in the winter of 2016. I had moved to Seattle in Fall of 2016 at the urging of my heart. I honestly thought I would just move to

Seattle, as I did in Sept of 2016 and then immediately fall in love...I mean, that was the plan and part of the reason I moved to Seattle...because much like San Diego, my heart was "calling" me there and I assumed it had called me there to find my next soulmate too.

So, when I got to Seattle and started my job, I started looking for and becoming open to my next soulmate relationship...and I attracted a few random suitors here and there...nothing serious, and nothing even close to what I was looking for. Then I remembered (I forget things too) that I needed a new list for my soulmate this time around and proceeded to write my list again, pouring my heart out about everything that I wanted at this stage in my life (I was 46). And then I put the list away, went on with my life and waited.

About springtime 2017, I was talking to my mama about relationships and what was next for me and I made an off-hand comment/prediction (it startled even me because it just felt so...true) that I wouldn't be surprised if I was in love and in a relationship again by that fall. Summer came and went, then September, then half of October...that was when my internal alarm bell went off...like HEY why isn't he here yet!? Oh shit, I may not fall in love this fall, I may not find my soulmate! What should I do next? Honestly, I really didn't know what to do next and when that happens, I often pray for guidance...like yoohoo...show me the next step please...need a lil help here. Thanks!

The "help", unbeknownst to me, came in the form of an email with an advertisement for an online dating platform that spoke to my deeply spiritual, organic, granola-y and woo-woo nature. I researched it and decided to sign up for their trial period. I started filling out the online profile info only to stop about half-way through, I felt discouraged...thinking this isn't going to work. The next morning, I got one of those marketing type emails from the dating site...but what it said must have gone straight to my heart, because it gave me the kick in the pants and spurred me on to finish my online profile. The headline of the email..."your tribe is waiting for you." Little did I know how prophetic that phrase would be.

So, I joined for free for 3 days to see what it was like, and I started getting winks or likes or whatever the hell they do (I can't remember now) and I started chatting with a few guys and overall, I just liked the vibe I was getting in there.

I had done some light online dating from a few of the bigger free sites in the past without much luck. So, I ended up committing to their 3-month package, which I think was like $29.99 at the time. Their idea was that people who invest (like actual $$) in finding love got better results and that the higher caliber people were the ones actually paying for online dating, so that is who you would meet by investing as well...'cuz like attracts like.

And I can absolutely say that is what happened for me. I chatted/emailed with several "good" men that were within my dating parameters during my time on there. And ultimately 3 men made it over my hurdles and met my criteria enough that they earned an in person coffee date with me (yes, I said "earned" a date with me and you will too!...more about why that is super important in a later chapter) and the 3rd time ended up being the charm for me as my soulmate came swooping in with his blast of bright, happy, loving, and generous energy.

He was actually outside the dating parameters that I had set for age (he was 14 years younger than me)...so he actually found me...I had attracted him! Within 2 weeks of joining, committing to, and investing in this online platform, we had started chatting and we had our first date about 3 weeks after I joined. Thank God for that stupid marketing email! We moved in together after only 8 months of dating and have been growing, evolving, and loving each other more and more ever since. He is my soulmate and the perfect guy for me at this stage in my life, we absolutely adore each other, and are rocketing each other towards our dreams. Time will tell if he is a "reason", "season" or a "lifetime" soulmate...I only get to know that in hindsight.

My story illustrates the power of how listening within, creating an intentional, comprehensive list and combining that with inspired, consistent action...will get you results. All of which I will teach you exactly how to do in this book.

The pivotal moment for me came when I learned that combining these 3 elements is what ultimately brought my soulmate speeding towards me and into my life. I wrote this book and put together the exact steps I took to get there, for you. I want you to learn these lessons (that took me years to discover through trial and error) in a fraction of the time it took me, find your soulmate quickly and joyfully and get on with living your dream life together. You've waited long enough...let's show you the ropes.

The Magic Soulmate Process

*Someone, somewhere is looking for exactly
what you have to offer.*
~Louise Hay

*H*ere is a brief overview of what we are going to cover in this book using the SOULMATE process to get you, step by step, to your own soulmate:

1. Step 1– **S**acred commitment to yourself - You will become aware of your own "why" and the important reasons for embarking on this journey at this stage/age in your life and why you will be successful this time.

2. Step 2 – **O**pening to the magic - You will begin to understand the importance of creating a comprehensive list of the qualities your ideal soulmate possesses and why this is the most important step in bringing your soulmate into your life.

3. Step 3 – **U**nderstanding your best dating platforms - You will understand the importance of listening to your intuition as you research and then choose the best dating platform for yourself and why this is the 2nd most important step in bringing your soulmate into your life.

4. Step 4 – **L**et's go all in together - You will join an online dating site that is aligned with your heart and feels safe and then create an authentic profile, so you can more

quickly, easily, and joyfully attract your soulmate into your life.

5. Step 5 – **M**ake him beg to earn a date with you - You will utilize a safe and proven series of dating steps that will help you save time and choose only the right men for you. You will understand the basics of online dating safety and have several safety nets in place for yourself as you date.

6. Step 6 – **A**sking for the right kind of support – You will create a support system for yourself as you go through this process and will understand the difference between the right kind of support and the wrong kind of support for this journey and choose accordingly.

7. Step 7 – **T**weaking your list, profile or platform - You will understand that this is a learning process and will see clearly how effective your list and profile are working based on the people you are attracting, you will then be given guidelines to tweak/adjust your list and profile and/or platform accordingly. You will know exactly how and when to re-align and make changes to your list, profile or platform in the face of set-backs.

8. Step 8 – **E**ver after: How to know if he is your "happily" - You will be given tools to learn exactly how to tell if a guy is Mr. Right, Mr. Almost Right, or Mr. Wrong and not waste a single minute on the Mr. Wrongs for you.

9. Resistance and Upping your Game - You will discover that through this process, you will have to deal with some self-doubt and both internal and external obstacles to being successful. Yet, you will begin to believe that progress towards your soulmate is not only possible but can even be fun during this process as you follow the steps and utilize the supportive and intuitive tools that are given to you. You will finally understand

that having a soulmate in your life is no longer a question of "if" but "when."

Elizabeth Ward

The Soulmate Process

Elizabeth Ward

Step 1 – Sacred Commitment to Yourself

I cannot remember exactly the first time
your soul whispered to mine,
but I know you woke it.
It has never slept since.
~ J.M. Storm

So, I will begin by asking you some of the same questions I ask my clients. **Why now? Why is now the right time for you to find your soulmate?**

For each of you, the answer will be different. For my client Mary, she identified that she was afraid of being hurt again, but she wasn't going to let this fear stop her from finding this special relationship in her life. Because a deeper part of her feels that she has this great love in her heart to give and to share in this special way, with a soulmate.

For many of you, a common thread I have heard again and again, is that you are generally happy in your life and being on your own. You have created a good group of supportive family and friends and are generally content in your life. Many of you have gotten to a point in your career where you have achieved many of the goals you set out to achieve, you have created security, and in some cases even wealth beyond your wildest expectations. And now you are wondering...what's next? And further...you are wondering if life could get even better if you allowed yourself this next level of love in your life.

Some of you have fears of losing your independence and getting hurt again and yet through it all are still hopeful, that by attracting a soulmate relationship, you can finally go beyond the pain and suffering of past relationships. That this time, and in this way, you can finally get it right.

Another question I often ask my clients is: **In what ways have you recently made space in your life for your soulmate?**

Mary identified that along with shedding a few extra pounds, she had recently been letting go of excess clutter in her life thus making extra space in her closet (for her soulmate's clothes).

For Gemma, she realized that not only had she recently ended the casual relationship, but she had also drastically decreased her emotional investment in work over the past year and had greatly reduced her work hours, all of which, she realized as we were working together, was an unconscious preparation (creating space) for her soulmate to come into her life.

For me, the space always came in the form of me literally shedding my old life and moving to another state (both of them on the west coast) that was more aligned with who I was on the inside, that quickly brought my soulmates into my life.

Also, I ask: **If you are successful in following these steps how will things be different a year from now and how will you know you have succeeded?**

For most of you, the answer is that you will have your soulmate in your life and be living it joyfully with him, maybe making plans to move in together, get married, or perhaps even starting a family together. One of the benefits of being over 40 is that you know yourself and what you want so well...so why wait? You are no longer willing to waste time on maybes.

Gemma saw herself Christmas shopping together with her soulmate next year and another client, Cindy saw herself walking on the beach hand in hand with her soulmate next year.

What you know is that success for you means that you finally have that special someone in your daily life who is your special person to lean on, to talk to at the end of the day and wake up with each morning and drink coffee together. And that you are finally beginning to build that life together, happily and joyfully.

For me the 'why now' questions always came from a deep listening within. And it usually came in the form of a whisper in the deep of winter, signaling that it was time to put myself out there and date again. Remember, with my first soulmate relationship, I had moved to San Diego and had been consciously/unconsciously looking for "him" and it wasn't until I had settled in about a year there that I heard "the call." It was time for me to date...so I did...slowly, haltingly, unsuccessfully, until I finally made my list which caused him to "show up" in my life 8 weeks later.

With my second soulmate, again I had moved to Seattle and had begun to consciously/unconsciously look for "him." I had settled in about a year there and had already made my list the previous winter, so I was ready. But this time, I needed to take that final step and actually date again in order to put me in the way of life's magic. I needed to take deliberate action towards him.

In the first scenario, I was taking deliberate action by dating but not being intentional about what I wanted, and the moment I got intentional with exactly the kind of man I was wanting in my life (by making a list) the universe delivered quite quickly....in only 8 weeks.

In the second scenario, I was being deliberately intentional by having a list, but not taking action and just hoping/wishing/praying he would show up. And the minute I took action and started dating, he showed up even quicker, in only 3 weeks.

Ultimately, I learned, it was the combination of intentional asking (by making a list) and consistent, inspired, deliberate action that created the magic. And that is exactly what I am going to show you how to do in this book.

And finally, the bigger "why" for me in all of this was simply this deep inner feeling/knowing that this kind of relationship was absolutely for me, even though I had no idea how to get it, achieve it, or attract it when I first started this journey in my 20's.

I think the same is true for you too, you were drawn to and picked up this book, because at some level there is this persistent yet gentle nudge from deep in your soul that says "yes...with all my heart, this is for me too."

The last thing I ask of my clients and I suggest for you is to get quiet, go inside and make a sacred commitment to yourself for how long you will stick with this process to find your soulmate...for most it is at least 6 months to a year. For others it is until they have their soulmate in their life. What will it be for you?

Step 2 – Opening to the Magic

What you seek is seeking you.
~Rumi

*I*n this chapter, I am going to teach you how to write an intentional list that will attract your soulmate to you lightning fast. You write a list for 2 reasons: 1. To put your "order" in to the Universe. Writing a list gives you something to focus on, so you start attracting what you want instead of attracting what you don't want or attracting by default. 2. To have something to refer back to when you start dating, to see how closely they guys you are attracting are a match for your list.

Think of it like this...if you were in a restaurant and they had a 12-page glorious menu of delicious food choices...you wouldn't just order food. You would order a filet mignon, with baby carrots and braised broccolini in a creamed butter sauce, with herbed garlic mashed potatoes with rosemary. You would order a lovely Cabernet to begin with and enjoy some crusty sourdough dipped in olive oil with parmesan. Get it? By not making a list, you are essentially saying..."I just want food...any food will do." You have to put your order in to the Universe and 1. be as specific as possible, 2. always frame it in the positive of what you want versus what you don't want, and 3. Write it in the present tense...as if it is happening right now. When you do these 3 things, the Universe will go to work immediately on your behalf to bring you exactly what you asked for.

Guidelines:

Your list must be phrased in the present tense...as if it is happening now and in the positive of what you want. To go back to our analogy of ordering food...you would never tell the waiter all the things you don't want on the menu when ordering...would you? This same reasoning applies to writing your ideal soulmate list to the Universe...so it can fulfill your order. When you are clear in your asking, the Universe will respond by being clear in its giving. So instead of saying I don't want him to be a liar...you say he is honest and trustworthy.

Write your list as if you are telling your best friend all about him. If you are stuck on what to write, just imagine you are talking to your best friend on the phone, and you have already gotten everything you could every want in a man and you are telling her all about how great he is (in the present tense, with positively framed statements).

When in doubt you can also write a blanket sentence statement that covers the essence of what you want to attract. Blanket sentences are more general but cover many bases in one fell swoop. If you are having trouble focusing on the specifics, **get in touch with the essence of the quality you would love in a soulmate** and write that down instead. Using this technique is also a good way not to get too attached to the minor details of your soulmate and let the Universe work its magic. For example, you can say he is 6'2", with brown hair, and blue eyes or you can choose a blanket statement by saying, "I am very attracted to him on all levels and he fulfills all of my physical wants and needs in every way." Do you see the difference? The 2nd statement covers the "essence" of what you really want by saying he looks a certain way...what you are really saying is that you want to be very physically attracted to him. When in doubt...get underneath the details and go for the essence of what you want in a soulmate. Got it? Good.

To begin writing your list: at the top of the page: State...*I am so happy and grateful that my soulmate has come into my life, he is so perfect for me in every way*...

The very first sentence of your list must say something to the effect of...*He is single, available and ready for a long-term, monogamous, intimate, committed, soulmate relationship that leads to*...(living together, family, marriage, etc)

Then write the rest of your list using the following guidelines and categories:

Examples to start sentences
(in the present tense)

He is...

We are...

We love to...

I am...

It is so awesome that we...

I am so happy because we now...

Categories and example sentences
(to get you jump started)

Physical:

We have incredible chemistry and are very physically attracted to each throughout our long and happy relationship

I am having the best sex of my life...it is both meaningful and steamy and we orgasm together all the time

He is a considerate, and gentle lover who loves to please me sexually

He is clean and healthy physically and sexually, non-smoking, drug-free, moderate social alcohol use if any

We are physically affectionate with each other and love holding hands and he always gives me the perfect amount of physical affection for me

He is a great kisser, has a cute butt, and I love his big hands...we both find each other very attractive

He is within 5 years of my age (if that matters to you)

It feels like heaven in his arms when he holds me

He thinks I am gorgeous and tells me all the time

He is safe, has healthy boundaries and respects my boundaries always

Emotional:

He is emotionally mature, and I feel completely safe and secure expressing my emotions with him

He understands me completely, has my back 100%, and supports me wonderfully in both good times and in bad

He is a great listener, and a great conversationalist, and is both interested in hearing what I have to say and is interesting when he talks

He can't wait to marry me and tells me all the time how much he loves me

He absolutely adores me and is proud to be in my life and proud to have me in his, he loves showing me off because he thinks I am gorgeous

We are the loves of each other's lives, we fall in love so quickly and easily and our deep loving connection is so strong and familiar and lasts for many, many years to come...he feels like "home"...this is my best soulmate relationship yet

Mental:

He is intelligent, smart, logical, and college educated

We have wonderful, deep, meaningful conversations all the time

I love what he has to say and respect how he looks at and thinks about the world

He respects my opinions and listens to my feedback or advice

We communicate wonderfully and are able to talk easily about any topic together

He is so playful and funny, he has an amazing sense of humor and we laugh together all of the time

We bring out the best in each other so easily and effortlessly...we genuinely like, love and respect each other

Spiritual:

He believes in a higher power and our spiritual beliefs are highly compatible

He has faith and believes in God

He meditates and prays everyday

He is deeply spiritual, and we love discussing and exploring our spiritual growth together

He is on a similar spiritual growth path to mine

We have a deep soul connection and wonderful spiritual connection with each other right from the start

Financial:

He makes great decisions with money that I agree with and support 100%

We agree about money easily

He is debt free and has no alimony payments

We are financially secure, stable and make sound choices about money together

He is always so generous with me, buying me gifts, taking me out to dinner, bringing me flowers, he is such a gentleman in all ways

Family and Friends:

He genuinely likes my family and friends and enjoys spending time with them

My family and friends accept my soulmate exactly as he is and he fits in easily with them

His friends and family love and accept me exactly as I am and we enjoy spending time together

He has an amicable relationship with his ex (he most likely will have one) and has his kids on the weekends only

We start a family together and/or our families come together and combine easily

I am happy to help raise his 2 children even if they are very young

His children are grown and out of the family home

He loves pets and our fur children are best buddies as we blend our homes together to become a happy non-traditional family unit

He always helps me around our home, running errands or helping with chores or feeding the kids and he makes our home so much better in so many wonderful ways

Career (His and Yours):

He makes great money in a fulfilling job he loves

He supports me in my career fully

We both have great work-life balance, so we have plenty of time to spend together

He is happy to support us financially as I pursue a new dream career

Culture/Ethnicity:

We have very compatible beliefs, viewpoints and ways of living, eating, and socializing that create overall happiness and harmony in our relationship

Social Activities:

We love doing so many of the same things together... (i.e. sports events, yoga retreats, dinners out, quiet nights in together, walks in nature, parties, church, etc)

We have very similar energy levels, social styles, and interests

Travel:

We love traveling together and are great travel partners...travelling often to wonderful places

We travel a few times a year to beautiful places that we both love visiting

Examples of "blanket" sentences to cover all bases:

We are incredibly attracted to each other and compatible on all levels: physical, emotional, mental, spiritual, sexual, financial, family values, social...etc

We have very similar interests, values, views, and opinions about life

We bring out the best in each other on all levels, we get along so easily and effortlessly

He is my best friend, my person, my soulmate, my intimate partner and we are so in love

We adore each other equally, love spending time together and laugh so much...we are having so much fun together doing everything we love

We love and accept each other deeply on all levels, bring out the best in each other easily, and are highly compatible in all areas of our life.

Things to think about or add to "flesh out" your list:

- Add 10 or more character qualities about him that you love: i.e. he is...respectful, honest, trustworthy, loyal, committed, playful, great sense of humor, man of his word, great work ethic, man of integrity, great listener, affectionate, generous...
- Think about all the things that have worked for you in your or other relationships and add those to your list in the present tense as positive statements.
- Think about all the things that have *not* worked for you (like bad kisser, chews with his mouth open, cheating, addictions, too serious, etc) and reframe in the positive.

- Think about deal breakers for you (cheating, drugs or alcohol abuse, kids, pets, living too far away, living at home with mom, workaholic, lying, etc) and then reframe in the positive. Ex: Cheating = he is loyal and monogamous sexually with me, he values our committed relationship. Workaholic = I am his #1 priority, he has a great work life balance, we spend the perfect amount of time together for me.

- Think about any quirks you may have (like having to live on the 2nd floor, excessive farting, burping, eating yogurt with a fork, leaving long VM messages) and reframe in a positive. Ex: He loves and accepts all my quirks and thinks they are adorable.

- Make your list about 2 pages long, you can type it or write it in a special journal

- Leave nothing out, if you leave it out...the Universe will leave it out (many years ago I wrote a list and attracted a guy to date and after a few months I noticed we were not falling in love, and when I looked back at my list, sure enough, I noticed that I had left out "we are in love"...so the Universe did too)

- You can either write a bulleted list in the present tense or you can write a story about your life together from the perspective of a year in the future and you are telling your best friend the story about how wonderful he is and all of his positive qualities, all of the good things he has brought into your life, all of the things you are doing together now, and all of your plans for the future. Either way...they both work

- Whenever possible, give your positive statements even more zazazing with adjectives like joyful, playful, happy, easily and effortlessly, all the time, love, perfect, heavenly, sexy, deeply, magically, fulfilling, etc...

- Make sure you explicitly ask for: a soulmate, monogamy, an intimate relationship (i.e. sex), long-term relationship, commitment and anything else that is a must have for you like family, marriage, living together, pets, etc.

- Always finish your list with...*This or something even better came to me so quickly, easily and effortlessly, the whole process was a complete joy, the timing was perfect, and it is a complete win/win situation for all involved.* (The "something even better" than my list showed up with my soulmate having 2 wonderful cats (I love cats and mine had all passed away), and him being an avid nature photographer with a kick-ass camera (I am an amateur nature photographer too and love nature pics). These little extras are how the Universe winks at you and shows you it is listening and has your back....it adds the whipped cream and dark chocolate sprinkles on top of your favorite coffee drink. When you notice these fun extras in the men you are attracting, it is a sure sign that the Universe's hand is in on it. The Universe can't help but to take everything you ask for and make it even better than you could imagine and also sprinkle in some magic for good measure.

- Have a trusted friend go over your list with you to make sure you have covered all the major areas in your life that are important to you and that the energy you are attracting with your list is what you actually want. With my clients, I go through and do a line by line edit of their list with them, to help them get even clearer, add a bit more sparkle or zazazing, and to give them feedback of the kind of guy I am sensing energetically from their list, so we make sure it is a match for the man they want to show up.

- Finally, pick a "soulmate song" that represents your list and how you feel about him and your future life together. And then listen to that song as you read through your list, visualize your life together and connect with his energy.

Remember, you have been single and content, living a full and happy life on your own for a while now...your life has been working...you don't need this, you want this and are choosing this relationship, at this time in your life. It's important to remember that you absolutely want this relationship to be way better than being single. Otherwise, why do it...right? Just by attracting this book you have shown that you are ready. He will add so many new and positive dimensions to your life that it will be almost astonishingly better than before. The ultimate goal is this...your life is so much better, more fulfilling, happier and richer in all areas because he is in it.

Step 3 – Understanding your Dating Platform Options

A soulmate is an ongoing connection with another individual that the soul picks up again in various times and places over lifetimes. We are attracted to another person at a soul level not because that person is our unique complement, but because by being with that individual, we are somehow provided with an impetus to become whole ourselves.
~ Edgar Cayce

This step involves doing some online research into the best way for you to attract a soulmate into your life.

First, type these words (or some variation that fits your life) into a search engine:

- Best dating sites for women over 40, 50, etc
- Best online dating for spiritual women over 40
- Best dating sites for professional women 40+, 50+
- Best way to date when you (your interest) after 40
- Best dating sites for sensitive people over 40, 50, etc

Look them all over, read about them, do your research to satisfy your brain and then choose the top 3 that you are most drawn to. Then...hold each one to your heart and ask if this is the best platform for you at this time to attract your soulmate...and notice how your heart feels. If it is the right place you will usually feel a "yes" or happy, light, relaxed, peaceful, or somehow inspired.

What you are looking for here is a match energetically with similar like-minded people...because if you are drawn to it, he will be too. You want to be surrounded by your tribe...your peeps...so your likelihood of attracting your soulmate will increase. Remember he is drawn to and loves everything about you already...you are his ideal soulmate and he is yours. You are doing similar things in your lives already. Your job is simply to do more of what you love and to choose a dating platform that feels "familiar" and resonates with you.

With my second soulmate...I had my list written but had balked at joining an online dating site since I hadn't had luck in the past...then "by chance" I came across a dating site that was advertised in a daily inspirational email that I receive and after looking into it and reading their FAQ's, etc it just felt so...right and everything they were saying was resonating with me. So, I joined for free for 3 days to see what it was like and I ended up committing to their 3-month package. Which ended up making all of the difference...because it was me investing in committing to finding him, instead of just waiting around for him to magically show up. Their stance was that people who actually invested (payed $$ for a dating site vs. joining a free one) in finding love got better results. And I can absolutely say that is what happened for me.

My second soulmate came swooping in with his blast of bright, happy, loving, and generous energy within 2 weeks of joining and we had our first date about 3 weeks after I joined. We moved in together after only 8 months of dating.

This is why it is so important to find the right dating platform for you...that is a match for your energy...because it will be a match for him too and speed this process along exponentially. By you choosing a dating platform that aligns with who you are on the inside, your guy kinda gets pre-vetted for you.

So ask yourself...what you would love in a dating site?
Which one feels like a match for you...on the inside?
Which one is resonating most with you right now?
What just feels right, even though you can't explain why?

You can join an adventure group for singles, a church group for singles, online dating sites, speed dating, a bowling league, hire a matchmaker...it doesn't matter...the point is that you need to be taking consistent action towards your soulmate while in alignment with what feels right to you. And if you choose to volunteer or join a group in order to meet like-minded people, you need only do things you love and are naturally drawn to...because like attracts like. By doing so, you multiply the Universe's power to create magic and speed your soulmate into your life. And let me tell you, I am learning there is a dating platform for everyone. Mary found a dating platform for Classical Music Lovers and Cindy found a new one for coffee lovers.

If you love gardening, join a group or do something with others that has to do with that, instead of doing something solely for the purpose of meeting other singles. If you can find a way to combine the two...dating and doing what you love, more power to you. I remember meeting a couple that both had a love of orchids and ended up meeting, dating, and ultimately getting married because they met through a group they had both joined for orchid lovers. Doing what you love not only makes you happier and more fulfilled...it makes you even more magnetic to your soulmate.

Some of my clients have asked...Do I really have to date and join an online platform? Well let me ask you this...if your car was broken down...would you go to the park to get it fixed? Would you sit at home, night after night with a broken car, hoping, wishing, or praying a mechanic would show up at your door? No, you wouldn't...you would go to the place where they fix cars!

It is the same with finding your soulmate...you online date or join groups of like-minded people or go to meetups or whatever 'cuz that is where the single people are! Now in our other scenario...sure you *could* meet a mechanic to fix your car at the park, maybe...and he *could* show up and magically knock on your door and offer to fix your car for you, someday. Miracles do happen for sure. But your chances of getting your car fixed are infinitely higher if you go to where the car fixers actually are!

It is the same with soulmates...you have to go where the single people are, the ones who are actually available and have signed up and are raising their hand saying YES they want to date and be in a relationship. Make sense?

I have heard of people meeting their soulmates when they joined a bowling league, at church, and even while volunteering at the food pantry. The point is not only to go where the single people are but to also do more of the things you LOVE to make it easier to meet like-minded people with similar interests to you. So, one of your options might be joining a group along with online dating...which is fine...so long as it is a step towards your soulmate in some way and you are taking consistent action in that direction.

I would have never met my second soulmate if not for finding and then investing in that online dating site...our paths would never have crossed while I was waiting for him to magically show up at my work. He lived an hour and a half away, across a body of water at the time. But the minute I took action (i.e. got myself to where the single people are) mountains moved very quickly....I only went out on 3 actual in-person dates (I will teach you how to streamline this process too, so you won't waste any time on men who are not a fit) and then my soulmate and I were exclusive and moving forward together. The same magic is available to you. Let's keep going.

Elizabeth Ward

Step 4 – Let's Go All in Together

*In all the world, there is no heart for me like
yours. In all the world, there is no love for
you like mine.*
~ Maya Angelou

Once you have researched and chosen your top 3 online dating sites, put them on a pad of paper in front of you and label them 1,2,3. Then close your eyes and place a hand over your heart center. Then run each choice by your heart and notice out of your top 3, which one:

1. your heart is most drawn to...
2. just seems like a good fit right now...
3. brings you peace, joy or just uplifts you...
4. feels the best overall even though you can't explain why...

Sign-up - for the dating site your heart has chosen and barring any super weird circumstances, commit to it for 3 months. This will help you to get a real feel for the site and to see the measurable results you are getting on it and if you feel like it is a good fit based on the men you are meeting. I do not recommend switching platforms until after 3 months.

Choose – about 10 recent pictures from the past 6 months...where you are lookin' smoking hot...and include at least: 1 where you can see your eyes, 1 full body shot (no nudes ladies), 1 with animals (if they are an important part of your life), 1 action shot doing something you love to do (like hiking, at a baseball game, playing volleyball, etc), 1 shot in sunglasses (just 'cuz those glasses are awesome and you know it)...1 pic of you dressed up and lookin' good, 1 dressed down, hair in a pony tail, with a baseball hat on and your glasses on but still lookin super cute....1 having fun, 1 laughing, 1 laughing while having a fun adventure that you love to do.

Choose - and use a **mojo song** to lift you up before you write your online profile – you know the one I mean...when you listen to it, you can't help but get up and dance! You absolutely have to shake your bootie and do that lip bite thing...cuz it just makes you feel so f*ckin good! Like yeah, here I am, check me out, I am such hot sh*t....so watch out world...cuz here I come! That is the song to listen to again and again as your craft your authentic online soulmate profile...the one that makes you feel all that!

Write – your online profile while you are in a '10' space (i.e. just after you have listened to your mojo song): Start with where you are, it's ok if it's not perfect, answer all questions honestly, authentically and to the best of your ability right now, and you can always spruce it up and add more zazazing later as you get your feet wet and learn more. Just get it done...that is the goal.

Here are some tips and shortcuts:

When in doubt on how to answer, always be honest and authentic...but in a fun way. Here is my actual online profile intro that I wrote when I met my second soulmate:

I'm new to this...so here goes. I am a techie with a masters in Psych, love nature photography, am a complete and total food lover (but can't cook worth a damn) cat lover, deeply spiritual and also delightfully real (i.e I swear). I grew up in Chicago and have lived in San Diego, Portland, and now Seattle. It seems I loves me the PNW, sweet, funny, giving guys, awesome healthy food (bonus if you can cook), and great coffee, red wine and conversation.

P.s....I am a tall drink of water...I'd prefer you to be tall too.

Ask me about: Why deep questions rock my world...and why I love cats and sci-Fi movies but not sci Fi movies about cats...big difference...just sayin.

I especially enjoy: Meditation, creative writing, Rumi quotes, positive, happy, fun people, dark/edgy humor, and real conversations

In my free time I can be found: Relaxing, walking, enjoying simple pleasures, reading, writing, learning, growing, meditating, and just getting better at doing life.

What I am most passionate about: Lifelong learning, technology and innovation, making a positive difference in people's lives

Frame negative things into the positive: like "I am a terrible cook," turns into "I can reheat with the best of 'em and double bonus if you can cook." Or "I don't enjoy camping." into "I can glamp like a mofo." Get it? Be honest about your perceived shortcomings and turn them into something positive, light-hearted and fun.

Show 'em...don't tell 'em: Show him you are fun and what you enjoy doing by including action pics of you doing something you love where you are laughing and having fun doing it! Show him you are funny by being funny, snarky, quirky, etc in the writing portion of your online profile.

You are WAY more interesting than you think you are. If you need to, ask your friends about some of the cool things you have done through the years that could be included in the "something interesting about me" section of your online profile. For example, one of my clients, Cindy, actually snow-shoes (that is...she walks on the snow with those tennis racket thingies strapped to her feet) which I think is super interesting and she also knows random factoids about her favorite baseball team...we're talking like trivia level here. To her these are no big deal, but to her soulmate they are like catnip and will draw him to her like a laser beam. So, if you need to...ask one of your best friends about some of your "interesting things about me" factoids that you may be overlooking about yourself because they are "just normal" and no big deal to you.

It's ok to show him your best self and be honest about your likes and dislikes: (i.e. camping, pets, kids, smoking, drug use, etc). For example, I am not a big fan of camping (and I swear to God, every man on god's green earth loves to camp!) and smoking cigarettes is a deal breaker for me. So the gist is...if you don't like it and it is close to or is a deal breaker for you...I don't care how cute he is or how perfect he is in every other way...don't override what you really want and pretend it's ok. Cuz it's not...and you will get stuck camping with a smoker every weekend who is not your soulmate.

Also, here's a lil nugget to ease your mind, when it comes to your soulmate, **you won't have to compromise your values or settle for deal breakers**. If you do...he's not your soulmate.

Onward!

Step 5 – Make Him Beg to Earn a Date with You

*A soulmate is someone who has locks that
fit our keys, and keys to fit our locks. When
we feel safe enough to open the locks, our
truest selves step out and we can be
completely and honestly who we are; we
can be loved for who we are and not for
who we're pretending to be.
Each unveils the best part of the other.
No matter what else goes wrong around us,
with that one person, we're safe in our own
paradise.
~ Richard Bach*

Congrats, you made it through the first 4 steps, which can often be the most challenging and where some people want to give up. I'm glad you didn't give in to the temptation because you are so much closer now to your soulmate...closer than you have ever been before...so keep going brave soul. I believe in you!

In the first week, especially if you are nervous or new to online dating, you can take 'dating in person' off the table. The first few weeks can be just about dipping your toe into and testing the waters of your online dating platform by liking, smiling, winking, and some light chatting with potential men to show initial interest.

Then I suggest that after you both have shown initial interest, and maybe you even decided to reach out and ask him a question to get the conversation started... that you then wait for him to genuinely engage you (no one liners!), and show interest in you by asking you questions, sharing a bit about himself and responding in a manner and timetable that works for you (i.e. he addresses your questions or concerns directly instead of avoiding them, he responds promptly to chats, and keeps his word, etc).

Then show him you have high standards and respect yourself by asking him to adhere to these standards **before** you agree to meet him in person:

1. Stay within the safety of the online platform chat/email feature until YOU are ready to give him your personal phone #.

2. Insist upon texting and talking on the phone to get to know him for as long as it takes YOU to feel ready for an in-person meet.

3. Only when you feel ready to take the next step and meet him in person; find a safe, public place for you to meet in person, like a coffee house or a cafe. At this point you should be feeling fairly comfortable with him and have a good bead/feel for who he is as a person.

The order you progress with every potential guy should look something like this:

1. Chatting/emailing within online platform (to protect your privacy and safety)

2. Text messaging on personal phone or personal email (only when you feel comfortable going to this next step

and safe enough with him to give out your personal number or email address)

3. Talking on the phone to get to know him and see if you enjoy talking to him, the sound of his voice and if talking to him makes you feel even more attracted to him. Ladies we were born and raised in a time before all of this technology, when people used to actually talk on the phone...it's ok to insist upon it now...if he is your guy, he will understand and respect you more for it.

4. Meeting in person for a coffee date at a very public place. This is where you will see if you actually have physical chemistry, enjoy being with him in person and (let's be honest) if you want to kiss him, 'cuz you can't go any farther if you don't want to kiss him

5. Move on to actual dates with him and see how many more hurdles you can get through together (i.e. sex, friend and family intro, living together, daily life, etc)

Things to remember once you are online and connecting with potential soulmates

When you are going through the matches the site has for you, **learn to include some "Maybe" guys (as far as looks)** at this point in your liking or winking process. If a guy is only a "maybe" looks-wise, but there is just something, or even a few things in his profile that make you feel drawn to him, listen to that inner nudge and give him a wink of encouragement. Because a "maybe" guy can quickly become your "hell yes" soulmate once you get to know him. We all know that a guy that can make us laugh, carry on a great conversation, is a gentleman, is generous, respectful and considerate becomes much more attractive in our eyes once we see these traits in action while we are dating. So, stay open to 'maybes' at this point. My guy was a maybe when I first saw and responded to his online message, but after I got to know him and responded to his thoughtful questions, heard his voice, watched how consistent, respectful, generous, and kind he was to me and then met him in person and felt our amazing chemistry, he was a hell yes!

Their job is to push the gas pedal, yours is to pump the brakes. Your guy will respect your boundaries, what you are comfortable with and your timeline. It's not only ok to assert this, it's necessary to show him that you have high standards and are willing to stick to them because you respect yourself.

You are not desperate...you have plenty of time and there are plenty of great men out there, one of whom is your soulmate. There is never a shortage of great men (get your mind to a place of abundance about this) if your mind can think him up...he exists, he just will not exactly match the picture in your mind of him physically...his outer shell may be different than you were picturing and that is ok. The essence of him that you asked for by creating your list will be a match for him. I have found my lists to match my soulmates at about a 90% accuracy. The other 10% is usually silly things like him having a sexy accent, or being a certain height, or him being a gourmet chef that are the only things the Universe leaves out...and these are in no way deal breakers for me...they were just extra fluff...so no big deal. During this process you may be tempted to stop dating when you have found a man that matches 50-60 % of your list and you will be tempted to settle for less...don't. Your true soulmate is so worth it...and so are you.

You are essentially interviewing him to see if he is your soulmate. In a way, by dating and following these steps/guidelines you are essentially asking him to run an obstacle course and pass over hurdles for an opportunity to audition for the role of your soulmate. You can wink and encourage him, chat with him, share details of your life that you feel comfortable sharing, and then you wait to see how many hurdles he can pass to get the opportunity to meet you in person. It is important to note that he will be interested in getting to know you and very interesting to you as well. Be assured, that your soulmate will not only pass all of the hurdles, he will practically fly over them to get to you.

He wants to win you and earn the right to be your soulmate. Let him make the majority of the moves and remember that he wants to win you....it makes you more valuable to him.

You are not playing games, you are showing him that you have high standards and respect yourself enough to adhere to those standards and ask that he meet those standards. If he is truly into you and your soulmate, he will rise to meet those high standards and be happy to do it. Definitely do not play hard to get, that is not the point; ask questions, engage in an easy back and forth volley of questions and answers, do your part to keep the conversation going, like you would a friend whom you are getting to know. But if you find yourself doing *all* of the heavy lifting and all he wants to do is meet you in person and he is not listening to what you want...let him pass. He is not your guy.

You are the prize and the prize never pursues. You can wink, like, encourage him with little nudges, respond with authenticity to his questions and ask questions back of him, but ultimately he must pursue you. I know it sounds old-fashioned but there are years of DNA at play here. And men value what they earn...let him earn the right to date you and be your forever guy and soulmate by not settling for a guy who is only half-heartedly pursuing you while keeping his options open. When it's the right guy, your soulmate, you won't have to guess or wonder if he's into you or not; you will be too busy chatting, answering his text messages, getting to know him because he calls at the perfect times, having lovely dates with him (that he has planned out ahead of time to impress you) and having him plan future dates together, to even have time to wonder. Because he will absolutely want you in his life and will be crystal clear in both his words and actions to let you know.

Remember this phrase and repeat it to yourself often: **It only takes one and what if it's easy?** You will be "sorting through" men to see who is a fit and who is not at this point. Your list and the steps above will help guide this process and also help you not waste time on in-person dates with men who have not met the criteria above. There will be several men who will get to a certain hurdle and then flame out...this is a normal part of this process and these men are not your soulmate. Trust that and *trust the process*. And remember, that ultimately, it really only takes one right match and it can be easy. It only took me 3 weeks, it can be that easy for you too.

Be ok with rejection and remember that whatever level you are feeling rejected, chances are your guy is feeling double or triple that amount since they are the ones who usually have the role of reaching out to us first. Show a little compassion for how much rejection he probably had to deal with on his way to meeting you. Also, it is not personal.

All you have are his words backed up by his actions at this point in the game. So, listen to what he says and doesn't say. And watch what he does and doesn't do. Is he showing genuine interest in you? Is he making the effort to reach out to you, talk to you, keep progressing forward with you? Is he keeping his word about when he will call or text you? I had a guy who seemed really great during our first online chat, then he said he would call/text at a certain time and he was a day late...not good. I cut him loose. I had another guy make it to the phone call stage of the process only to talk about himself and his kids the entire time...not good. I passed on him too. This is all very normal and expected during this process.

Do your part by not pretending or over-compromising in the beginning and saying that you love sports or want to take care of his 5 children (when you don't) as this will lead to trouble later on...that is why you have your list and are putting your authentic self out there. There are plenty of great matches for your authentic self with all of your lovely quirks and unique wants without you having to try to be something you are not. Who you are is already awesome.

Be the person you want to date by being respectful of him too. If you are not interested, thank him and say that you are not interested. There is nothing wrong with being considerate, honest and respectful during this process. And it shows the Universe the kind of man you want to date by being those qualities yourself. For example, if you don't like when men play games, don't play games yourself. Be the person you want to date...if you are asking it of him, be willing to do it yourself.

When it's right you can do no wrong...and when it's wrong they can do no right. This is good to remember because it sums up what it is like when you meet and begin a relationship with your soulmate. They will say or do the right things at exactly the right times for you and you will do the same for them too. It will feel absolutely magical along with this incredible ease and joy when you are with your soulmate, like you have done all of this before and are picking up where you left off from another time. At some level he will feel familiar to you, he will probably smell amazing to you, and it will feel like heaven in his arms and like time stands still when you are together. You will have long magical conversations that make you feel like 5 minutes have passed when it really has been 4 hours. You will enhance each other's lives in every way even as your combined energy naturally encourages you both to grow, and to become more of who you are through your love and deep soul connection. It is one of the most magical connections I have ever felt in my life and it feels like the closest thing I have come to touching heaven here on earth. This magic is available for you too, that is why you attracted this book at this time, it is available to all who are brave enough to ask for this majestic bit of magic here on earth.

Step 6 – Asking for the Right Kind of Support

There are no accidental meetings between souls.
~ Sheila Burke

This may go without saying, but I'm going to say it anyway...you need the right kind of support during this journey to your soulmate. Why? Because it will change you in ways you can't yet see or even imagine and you are going to need someone (maybe even a few someone's) to talk to as you go through this deep inner process.

Chances are you have already begun to change the way you are seeing this journey, maybe you have made some noticeable changes, in the way you dress or eat, or maybe the changes are more subtle, like starting to actually look at your surroundings when you are at the grocery store, or the coffee shop, because in your bones you feel...different somehow, now that you have opened yourself up to your soulmate. You are beginning to realize that "He" could appear at any time, in any way, and anywhere, even outside of your dating platform.

Elizabeth Ward

**Here are the suggestions I have for you
at this stage of the journey**

You may be just winking, or chatting with a few guys in your online platform chat feature at this point or maybe things have progressed quickly and you are talking on the phone already...so here is what you need to set up next, for when a guy has aced all of your hurdles and has won an in-person meet with you at a coffee shop or public café.

You absolutely need a dating buddy to tell where you are going & when. You need to text them with your date's info (name and as much info as you know so far), where you are going and when, and then text when you are home safely after your meet. This step is invaluable and is *non-negotiable*. I trust and affirm that you are attracting great, safe, honest, and trustworthy men, because there are just so many of them out there...AND I want you safe in this process. Your dating buddy is your safety net. Think it over and ask one of your trusted girlfriends to support you in this...in all likelihood, they will be delighted to support in this special role.

You also need a close heart friend to "debrief" and talk to about all of the foibles and shenanigans of online dating. Chances are it has been a while since you dated and the dating world has absolutely changed since the last time you dated...guaranteed. It's a new world, and you will absolutely adapt to it and figure it all out. And as you do this, make sure you have someone you can talk to about it all if for no other reason than to help you process all of the new information and all of the changes you are making and ways you are growing during all of this.

Play your cards close to your chest with most people until well into dating your soulmate exclusively (like getting through your first trimester, before telling everybody). This may seem like you are being secretive, but hear me out. I absolutely

54

want you to **tell maybe 2 or 3 of your most trusted heart friends everything** that you are doing and going through in this process. But...with other acquaintances, family, work friends, etc that are not in your inner circle, just give them very broad and general info about what you are doing and then only if they ask. Why?

Because if they have never created a similar result or have not gone through something similar not only will they not get it, they will encourage you to settle. And here is the kicker, they will actually think they are helping you by doing this. Don't get me wrong, they absolutely mean well and they love you and think they are supporting you in their advice...they think they are keeping you safe from getting hurt. They don't realize that their discouragement or lack of belief in what you are doing actually hurts you more. It's ok, there are plenty of lovely friends that will support you and believe in you as you go after exactly what you want...focus on them and only give them the juicy details about this new amazing soulmate that you are attracting into your life.

Remember, you do not owe anyone any more information about your life than you see fit to give them. They do not have an automatic "in" to your life unless you are sure they are 100% in your corner and **supporting you in getting what you want**, which is your soulmate.

One of my clients, Cindy brought up the fact that many married women had tons of advice for her on how to attract a relationship or had set her up on blind dates where the only compatibility criteria seemed to be that they were both single. I am sure this has happened to you too, many long-time married folks just don't get it because this problem (finding your soulmate) was never their mountain to climb...and that's ok...just don't go to them for support as you take this step in your life. Everyone has their own mountain to climb, for some it's money, career, health...and for you it's a significant love relationship. No bigs. I am showing you the way...because I now know the way...it was my mountain to climb and I achieved the summit...twice. You will too.

Step 7 – Tweaking your List, Profile, or Platform

When deep down in the core of your being you believe that your soulmate exists, there is no limit to the ways he or she can enter your life.
~Arielle Ford

This is where you get to see the power of your list in what you are attracting and if you have any holes in your list. Every guy you attract is feedback from the Universe and each guy that is a 'no' will get you one step closer to your soulmate. For example, if you notice that all the guys you are attracting seem to be separated, but not yet divorced, you may have a "hole" in your list...so go back and make sure you have, "they are single, available and free from all past relationships" in your list.

Here are some more guidelines for you

If you notice that you are **attracting guys with a lot of drama**...add "He is low drama" to your list and make sure you are managing and reducing the drama in your own life. **Remember like attracts like, so the easiest way to fix**

something is to *be* that thing. If you are attracting guys who don't keep their word....add that to your list as a positive like "he is trustworthy, a man of his word and a man of high integrity in all ways" and then look at the areas in your own life where you don't keep your word, lie, or break your own integrity in situations.

Remember, **be the person you want to date**...if you are not healthy, don't expect him to be. You can expect you and he to be at about the same level in most areas of your life and how you do things...but that you each will have something (maybe several things) that you do about one step better than your soulmate, and these will be the areas of growth where you both can contribute to each other in positive ways. Remember, above all else, soulmate relationships offer the incredible opportunity for positive growth.

If you **aren't getting a lot of traffic** with the right men reaching out to you, and you want to re-vamp your online profile...before you do...STOP. Go back and read through your list, visualize your life together, and listen to your soulmate song to really get his vibe. Once you have done all of that, I want you to **"put on" or wear your soulmate as you read your online profile through his eyes**. From his perspective, what changes could you/would you make...if any?

Have a heart friend (someone you deeply trust to be honest with you) read your online profile and give you feedback about what the energy feels like that you are putting out there. Are you putting your '10' self out there? Or are you playing small for fear of looking full of yourself, exposure or letting your light shine too bright? If the feedback you get feels right, and authentic to who you are and makes your heart beat a bit faster because it is a bit outside your comfort zone...go ahead and make the tweaks. You are not here to keep doing what you have always done...that will just keep you where you have always been. You are here and reading this because your heart called out to you for something different, something more. So open up and do a little something different and become a little something more.

Before you make any changes/updates to your profile, ask yourself, **"Who is the woman who attracted this soulmate?"** And then to the best of your ability, "put her on" and write/make changes from her perspective.

If all else fails and you gave your online site a "**good old college try" for 3 months** and it just doesn't seem like a good fit or you are not getting the results you had hoped for...then you can go ahead and try another online dating site to see if it is a better "fit" for your energy and who you are looking for. Then try it out for 3 months using all of the same parameters from the first 7 steps in this process.

To put it in its simplest terms, **it all boils down to a numbers game**. You will go through X number of guys and by taking these steps and going through this process in the way that I have laid out for you...you will meet your soulmate. If you were buying a house or searching for a better job and if after 3 months you didn't get your ideal home or job, you wouldn't just give up and say, "well I guess it's not in the cards for me in this lifetime." No, you would keep focusing on what you want (your list), visualizing your life together as if it is already happening, feeling all of the good feelings as if it was already in your life, and taking action towards it in some consistent way. And, chances are, with each thing that didn't work, you would be getting better at that search too. Maybe trying different realtors, or job sites, and you would learn what is and what is not working, and you would adjust your course based on that.

I can guarantee that you have done this process before, in some other area of your life, when you attracted something "big" that you had never achieved before and that you weren't sure was even possible until you achieved it. Go ahead and remember that time now, remember how good it felt to achieve it, remember the steps you took along the way, the adjustments you made, and remember the doubt you had at the beginning, like "I have no idea how I am going to achieve this." The same tenacity and focus you applied when achieving those goals in other areas of your life is what is needed here, right now. I know you "think" it is different because it is soulmate love...I am here to tell you...it is no different. To the Universe, attracting a soulmate relationship is as easy as attracting a quarter. Get your head around that...and keep going chicky!

Step 8 – Ever After: How to Know if He is your 'Happily'

A soulmate is someone to whom we feel profoundly connected, as though the communicating and communing that take place between us were not the product of intentional efforts, but rather a divine grace.
~ Thomas Moore

So many people ask me...how do I know if he is "THE ONE?" (Cue dramatic music) and the good news is...it's much easier to figure out than you may think...let me show you:

He should be a match for at least 80% or more of your list, my two soulmates were at least 90% of my list. There was a great guy I dated just before meeting my second soulmate, and he was about 50% of my list, and I was definitely tempted to settle even though in my heart I "knew" we would never go the distance. You will be tempted to settle during this process...don't. You made your list for this very specific reason and it will guide you to know the truth when you need it most...trust the list.

Once you are dating exclusively, **you will keep passing hurdles and milestones together, almost effortlessly.** Like kissing, sex, meeting family and friends for the first time, you will have incredible compatibility on so many levels, you will have similar energy levels, and love of doing similar things and may even have very compatible rituals like Christmas, or a morning routine, etc. And you will just keep passing hurdles together until your relationship has run its natural course...whether that is a few months, a few years, or a lifetime. You only get to know why this particular soulmate came into your life and how long your relationship lasted, at the end. In other words, you only know if they are a reason, season, or lifetime soulmate at the end looking back.

One of you will do the right thing at the right time to keep you both moving forward together. I remember with my first soulmate, I actually tried to break up with him after about a month of dating. At the time I was kind of freaking out because he was so awesome and this small part of me was used to and felt safe and comfortable being alone and unloved. And because I was so uncomfortable and unfamiliar with this great new love, I tried to pull away and dump him. And thank God, he called me on my sh*t, and figured out that I was so afraid that he would hurt me (because I loved him so much and that made me feel vulnerable) that I was going to try and do it to him first. He was like, "Wait...so you're going to break up with me because you are afraid that I may break up with you and it will hurt?' And I was like...."yes." And then he said, quite resolutely, "Well...I'm not going to let you!" That was a huge defining moment in what was to become an incredibly significant 10-year relationship in my life. You will have several defining moments in the beginning of your soulmate relationship too....and one of you will step up to the plate and throw the love card so you can continue moving forward together.

You will discover as you date that **he will have several more surprisingly delightful nuggets that weren't on the list but that completely light you up and make him even more attractive to you.** For me it was discovering that my second soulmate had 2 gorgeous cats, that he was an avid nature photographer and because he knew I loved nature scenes too, would text me pics of gorgeous sunsets and landscapes throughout the day because he knew how much I loved them. Also, and this is a small thing...but to me it was huge. He texted in full sentences with correct capitalization, spelling, and punctuation. And if he made an error...he would correct it in the next text. I am such a stickler for good grammar so...I loved that! It is all of those little nuggets that he brings to the table that will add up to a great relationship together.

If you remember nothing else...remember this: **If it is right, you can do no wrong and if it is wrong, you can do no right.** In a very real way, you cannot miss each other or go past each other. Your list combined with the deliberate action you are taking to date means you will be in the way of each other...as if on a direct path to each other. As long as you are listening within and following where your intuition leads, you will do the "right" things and say all the right things to "your" guy. Barring outright rejection of him and flippin' him the bird...when it's your guy, you kinda can't get it wrong. Remember, I was tempted to stop dating when I met the guy (50% of my list) just before my soulmate, then for some reason he (50% guy) got a little flaky for a few days and that was all the opening the Universe needed to get my soulmate through. I remember how good his energy felt, it came through crystal clear, even in the online chat platform; I thought, this is a good, solid, salt of the earth guy with tons of enthusiastic energy. And I remember that I really wanted to talk to him, I felt inspired to talk to him, something about him just felt so...good. And, as icing on the cake, he found me. Because of his age (he was younger than me), he was actually outside of the age parameters I had set on the site, so he would have never come up on my radar as a possible match for me based on the algorithms of the site. But that didn't stop the Universe or my list from working...he still found me!

You will also be in exactly the right place at the right time for the two of you to meet and move forward together...trust that.

You will know because you will have done the following visualization (see below) so many times that he and **your life together will be so familiar to you that you cannot mistake him for anything but your soulmate.**

∞ ∞ ∞

Visualization –

Imagine a week in your life with your soulmate...

Begin with a Saturday morning, as you wake up beside him, what's the first thing you do? As you progress in your morning, what you are doing for breakfast? Do you go out, eat at home, eat with your whole family? After breakfast, what activities come next on a typical Saturday morning in your life together? How about lunch? What happens and who do you have lunch with on a typical Saturday in your life with your soulmate? What happens after lunch? Then dinner...do you dress up and go out for dinner and movie, or do you stay in and cook together? What about Saturday night? What are some of the things you do together on a Saturday night? As you wind down your day go through your night routine just before bed. Notice the feelings you have about your day. Notice any unique or surprising features that you didn't expect in your life with your soulmate. As you drift off to sleep, does he hold you close?

Then move on to Sunday and visualize what you are doing starting at breakfast...take yourself through a typical Sunday in your life with your soulmate. Breakfast, lunch, dinner, activities, friends, family, events, outings...what are you doing together? How do you feel about what you are doing together? Feel those lovely feelings fully.

Then move on to the work week and notice how the week flows. Do you leave for work at the same time, do you eat breakfast together? Does he bring you coffee in the morning cuz he knows how much you love it? Do you commute together to work? Does he text or call during your workday? What happens at lunch? Are you meeting a friend, or your soulmate? After lunch...what happens? What time do you both get home from work? What is a typical dinner during the work week? What do your evenings look like together...what do you do/not do during the week versus the weekends? Just notice all of the images you now have about a week in the life with your soulmate and revel in all of the feelings of contentment, fulfillment and happiness that visualizing this life together brings.

As you let yourself start knowing about your life together, remember that your soulmate most likely will not be an exact match for what you are picturing in your head, but **your guy will match the essence of your list and your visualized life together.** To illustrate my point, I remember when I was moving back to Chicago, and what I was visualizing (and on my list) was living near my sister in the suburbs, close to a library and close to a healthy food store and paying a specific amount of rent because I was starting grad school. The picture in my head was of the suburbs. And the Universe delivered me my list, but in the city, living near my other sister! Not only did I end up having a library right across the street, and a natural food market 1 block away. I got to live in the *same building* as my sister, just one floor above her and for the reduced rent (which is almost unheard of in the city of Chicago) that I needed while in grad school. So, the moral of the story, don't get overly attached to your guy matching the physical pictures in your head exactly...because he probably won't.

When I was picturing our life together, I imagined my soulmate to be a 6'5" African American man...but he showed up as a 6'1" white guy. Going back to my list...it said: "I want him to be bigger than me" and he was and, "we have incredible sexual chemistry and are attracted to each other and compatible on all levels...and we are. By being more general and asking for the essence of what I wanted, I actually gave the Universe more opportunities to fulfill my list requirements in unique ways. So my list worked...and yours will too as long as you let go of the pictures you have in your head about him.

You are not settling, you are absolutely expecting him to match the essence of your list (at 80% or higher) and match the essence of what you feel when you have been visualizing your life together. You are simply using your focused intention and taking baby steps towards this life and letting the Universe do the heavy lifting. Savvy?!

Important questions to ask yourself as you date:

- Do I feel uplifted by him? Do I feel loved, supported, understood, and heard?
- How do I look after spending time with him? Do I feel like my best self with him? Do I like who I am when I am with him? Does he bring out the best in me easily? How does my body feel when I spend time with him?

- Do I feel like more of myself or less of myself when I'm with him? Do I light up in his presence? If I look at pictures of myself while dating him, how do I look?
- Do I like who he is as a person? Do I like what he has to say? Are his words and actions congruent?
- Is there an ease between us? Do I feel joyful and uplifted in his presence?
- Is he supporting my best self? Does he encourage me to be or do better?
- Does he genuinely want the best for me? Am I more of who I am or less when I'm with him?

Here are some basic hallmarks to look for in a soulmate relationship:

- Highly compatible in major areas of your life, you will want the same or similar things in life, have similar energy levels, drive, ambition and values
- It feels like heaven in their arms and there is an ease to all your interactions, conversations and time spent together, like you have done this before and are just picking up where you left off
- There is an incredible opportunity to grow, change, evolve quickly and heal in deep ways, you may get triggered, it's ok, that is normal, just get some support from a heart friend who knows you and can help you re-center
- You will tend to bring out the best, and sometimes the worst, in each other
- You are essentially "the same in the middle", you will notice as you get to know each other that you have many similar stories, similar wounding patterns, and similar ways of coping with and seeing the world.

- Soulmates help each other move forward in significant areas of life. Soulmates spur each other's growth; whatever growth is needed in both of your lives at the time. Whether the growth is painful or joyful, do not doubt that when you call upon a soulmate to enter your life, significant growth will take place in a major area of your life. For example, my first soulmate helped me heal my past, in the 10 years we were together, he essentially "grew me up" and gave me many of the things I never got from my parents while growing up. My second soulmate helped me with my mid-life career transition, by believing in me, encouraging me and having my back in a way no-one has ever done for me.

Resistance and Upping your Game

People think a soul mate is your perfect fit,
and that's what everyone wants. But a true
soul mate is a mirror, the person who
shows you everything that is holding you
back, the person who brings you to your
own attention, so you can change your life.
~Elizabeth Gilbert

This is the go-to chapter for when you are feeling out of sorts or experiencing any self-doubt on your journey...come here and find the perfect little nugget to lift you out of any self-doubt funk you may be in. You will know exactly which one is for you because you will get chills and know that this is indeed the perfect message for you at this time.

Remember the 4 D's – chances are you are using one of these as a coping mechanism to avoid the uncomfortable/vulnerable feelings that go with putting yourself into a new situation such as dating. It becomes easier to focus on something familiar (even if it is unhealthy) to divert your attention to help "skiv off" uncomfortable feelings. When you are in the grip of one of these, you can easily get off course for months or even years. And the kicker is...they feel so compelling and real!

Here they are:

1. **Delay** – This is when you put something off *until*...with until being the keyword here...you tell yourself that you can't really go all in with this process *until* you lose the 20lbs, or *until* you get your finances in order, or *until* you get that medical procedure or *until* the holidays, vacation, or busy season at work are done...etc. You get it and you know if you do this one. It's a convenient way to put off what you are really wanting until a later date...that unfortunately never comes.

2. **Distraction** – This is the "oooo shiny" method of coping with uncomfortable feelings...where you suddenly find yourself enthralled with organizing your closet, or cleaning dog poop out of your backyard, redecorating your entire house, changing jobs or undertaking some massive new project. Or you may find yourself "checking out" by binge watching TV, movies, over-eating, drinking, socializing, or otherwise engaging in suddenly compelling and highly distracting activities that, before you decided to take this step and go all in to find your soulmate, had not interested you one iota.

3. **Denial** – This is the "I don't really need this" method of coping. This is where you invalidate your needs, trying to convince yourself that you are just fine the way things are...that everything in your life is working, you are comfortable, you don't really need to find your soulmate...this is no big deal. And you may go one step further and invalidate the steps and method in this book as well...by saying things like "she doesn't know

70

what she's talking about" or "this will never work" or "it can't be this easy" before you have even given it a try.

4. **Drama** – And finally, last but certainly not the least...I don't know why this is, but when you decide to step up and out into the unknown, out of your comfort zone and into a greater version of yourself, it's like you are suddenly a magnet for drama, either in your own life or your immediate friends and family's lives. I have seen this over and over again. And the temptation for you will be when this comes up (because at some level it will) to **not** jump into the rabbit hole and allow yourself to become mired down and distracted with the family and friends who are causing said drama and to instead stay focused forward. Can you still love them and show them that you care for them without derailing your own happiness and dreams? That will be your challenge as you progress forward into this positive, life-changing relationship that you are calling to you.

Choose a single word for the coming year...a meaningful word for you to focus on this year that supports you in finding your soulmate and being that woman who attracts this wonderful relationship into her life...put your hand over your heart and listen for the word...let it come from your heart and write it down and keep it where you can see it throughout the year. Then when you are off-kilter, use the word to bolster you, comfort you and get you back on track by helping you to focus on what you want...a soulmate relationship in your life.

Choose 1 inspirational quote or phrase that instantly re-centers you, that may also line up with the word you have chosen for yourself for the coming year. Put it where you can see it every day, along with your word. For example, my word for the year when I attracted my soulmate in 2017 was "soul love" and my quote was "Someone, somewhere is looking for exactly what you have to offer" by Louise Hay. Re-read your word and quote as often as possible to re-center and re-balance you during times of stress or self-doubt.

Invest in upping your self-care as you grow and take these steps – Remember, you are growing in a major area of your life, honor that and give yourself extra self-care and support for this process. When I was going through some of the changes that this level of relationship asked of me, I remember kinda griping about it, honestly. And as I was sorta pissing and moaning within, I heard my wiser self calmly ask: **"Did you really think you could get to the next level without having to up your game?** In other words, did you really think you could ask for this major change in your life and not have to change some things in your life too? Duh right?! This question immediately centered me and reminded me that I had called this relationship into my life, and that I was now responsible for upping my game and changing/growing to match the vibe this new relationship was asking of me. Not in a bad way, mind you, but at the time, it felt rather uncomfortable.

My small self liked the familiarity and comfort of the way things were...even if they were not fulfilling. Your small self, the one who is used to and feels comfortable with your life the way it is will absolutely protest and give you a hard time about making these changes in your life...this is not only normal, but expected. It thinks it is keeping you safe by keeping you small. Just know that...and don't let it win...don't let it keep you small. Up your game instead and repurpose that that small part of you by giving it a new job to do.

Ask yourself: **What's the worst that can happen if it takes longer than I think and failure is not an option?** At this stage of the game, if you have truly gone all in and invested yourself in this process then the question is not IF this will happen for you but WHEN this happens for you...feel that truth in your heart. Trust the timing to be absolutely perfect...because it will be.

Stand like a superhero - I learned about this in my psychology program and the gist is that the position of your body, and your posture affects your emotional state. For example, when you sit slouched, head down, shoulders hunched without smiling, this can induce a state of feeling low or depressed. Just like smiling for 20 seconds can create a feeling of happiness, it's the muscles in your face triggering the memory and pathways of happiness.

Right now...right this very instant, stand up, spread your legs wide, fist your hands on your hips, puff your chest out, lift your chin and look up into the sky and off into the distance. Imagine that you are on a very high mountain top surveying your life and all the good you have already created in your life. You're strong now and you hold yourself in this position, with your hands on your hips, your chest puffed-up and raised, your chin lifted high because you remember how strong you have been and your incredible bravery as you have faced and overcome the many challenges throughout your life. You are a fu*king superhero god-blessit!

Feel the power, giggles and strength surge through you as you stand in this pose for at least 3 minutes...Or for as long as it takes for you to remember your own superpower strength. When I do this exercise during my program, there is always so much surprised and delighted laughter at how such a simple exercise can create such a powerfully positive shift in mood in the whole room.

Imagine it like it is happening now – just before I met my second soulmate, I would lay in bed at night and imagine his arms around me, holding me and how good that felt with him in bed with me. About 3 weeks later, that vision came true. Gemma imagined walking in the door after work, coming home to him, and he's there cooking and then they are walking the dog together in the neighborhood later that evening. Mary imagined his clothes next to hers in the closet. You too can imagine him into the everyday areas of your life right now. Imagine him shopping with you during the holidays and being next to you in pictures with you and your family or having coffee in the morning with you.

It's Ok to take breaks as you need to – during this process honor your energy, your timeline and your need for downtime as you go through this. Take a weekend off...then come back to it with fresh eyes and perspective...time away is ok...just come back and keep taking those baby steps forward.

When in doubt, you can also do this:

- Listen to your soulmate song and visualize your life together and how good it will feel to be together
- Read through your list, trust your list, love your list, trust the process
- Listen to your mojo song and do something that makes you feel delightful
- Remember a day/week in your life with your soulmate visualization and revisit that again and again
- Remember this...It only takes one and what if it's easy? What if the whole process could not only be low drama...but a total joy as well? In the end, it really only does take one right fit...and it could be easy...so why not?
- Ask yourself...Why not Me? Other people have achieved this...why not me too?
- Watch for signs and make note of them as positive progress – I have a client who, in the past when she was

manifesting a large sum of money, something she had never done before, kept a list of all of the positive signs along the way and any money that came to her in the process. Sure enough, about 6 months later she had achieved the financial goal that she was focusing on. The same principles will work for you with your soulmate. Look for all the ways you see men "popping up" in your life. After going through this process, another client posted a pic of themselves with a sunset in the background and another interesting thing too...there was a guy in the background. She hadn't even noticed...but I did! These are the positive signs I am talking about...they are the playful ways the Universe tells you that it has heard you. They matter...make note of them and give thanks for them and more will come until one day it will be him, your soulmate, in the picture beside you, smiling down at you, his arm wrapped lovingly around your shoulder.

- Think of other things you've manifested in the past and the steps it took to get there, this is no different than that. You have absolutely had success in another area of your life where you achieved an "unknown" even though you didn't know how to do it. It is the same process with this and of course you will be successful!

- Ask yourself: Who is the woman that overcomes this obstacle and gets what she wants? Be that woman and act as she would act when faced with dilemmas about what to do...act as her...come from her way of thinking and being in the world...take the actions she would take.

Visualization
...to use when you have a block

You're at the beach, sitting in front of a beautiful fire, you look into it and let it hypnotize you as you call to mind the negative emotion you are feeling. As you gaze into the fire and call the block to mind, you ask your intuition: Where does this come from? Then you reach into your back pocket and you pull a picture out, then you notice who or what is in the picture, what stands out the most about the picture, and what do you feel as you look at the picture?

Then flip the picture over, there is a message on the back. You read it and take the message into your heart. And when you are ready, you let the picture go into the fire, realizing that this is just a story from your past, that you believed was true but is no longer helpful and needn't continue to be a part of who you are.

You let that story go now, giving thanks for the lesson...you throw it into the fire. And you remember in your heart, that you have always been more than this small story of who you are. You are now ready to be more of who you really are.

Remember to have fun with this – for f*cks sake...you get to update your underwear and get some fun new outfits for this "new you" that you are introducing to the world. Also, when a wonderful man has made it through the steps and has earned an in-person date with you, it's so much fun getting treated to dinner, having a man wine and dine you, and exploring the world together on your new adventures...enjoy it as much as possible.

I said that I would tell you **the real reason you have not attracted your soulmate until now**. But first, I want you to sit with this question in your heart and get very honest...now ask yourself: **What is the *real* reason I have not yet attracted a soulmate relationship into my life?**

Here is what I have learned on my journey with this...you have to be **all in**; with time, money, energy, and focus...it's that simple. What I know now is that investing all of yourself in solving this problem is the single most important thing you can do to be successful and achieve a soulmate relationship. Because some infinite part of you knows and feels your total commitment and the Universe then responds in kind.

The Universe doesn't like half measures, it's like you are putting in two different orders...like saying you want to eat steak and eat vegetarian at the same time...that is why you have been getting mixed results until now.

- The more you invest in yourself and go **all in** (time, money, focus, energy) the better your results will be...keep this as your singular focus until it is achieved...and it will be.
- The Universe knows when you are all in (money, energy, time, focus) and responds in kind

Final Question: Ask yourself: What is the most surprisingly delightful thing you learned about yourself on this journey? Then drop into a light meditative state and ask your heart the same question. Notice if/how the answers are different from your head versus your heart.

Elizabeth Ward

My Wish for You

What greater thing is there for two human
souls than to feel that they are joined to
strengthen each other, to be at one with
each other in silent unspeakable memories.
~ George Eliot

You made it to the end of this book, and I am so proud of you for having the courage to take this journey with me, to open yourself up in new ways and put yourself out there, outside of what you have always done and outside of your comfort zone. You went ALL IN and invested in yourself, with me as your guide, on this journey of your heart. You followed the steps, got clear about what you wanted, took action, and trusted the process to work.

Chances are that through the years, like me, you happened to do one or even a few of the steps, randomly, that were outlined in this book. And because you didn't get results like you saw so many of your friends or family achieving in this area, you may have incorrectly concluded that something was wrong with you or that this was somehow 'not in the cards' for you. Nothing could be further from the truth. Just because you were a good observer but a poor interpreter of what you were seeing doesn't make the belief true. You now know better...so you will absolutely do better. There was never anything wrong with you...only your method. It was simply incomplete until now.

If you have finished reading this book and are actually implementing the ideas in this program...let me assure you that a soulmate relationship is in your near future. If it wasn't possible for you to have this level of relationship, it wouldn't even be a blip on your radar. It would never have come into your consciousness as a longing or a discontent in the first place. For this reason alone, a soulmate relationship is *absolutely* for you. Once your heart and soul have announced your desire to the Universe for this magical relationship, there is no going back to the bland, disconnected and casual relationships of the past. The question is no longer *if* your will find your soulmate...but *when*.

And this book **is proof** that a loving Universe that has heard all of the secret longings in your heart and made sure you would find this exact book at this exact time in your journey. If you are reading this book, then it is not too late to find your soulmate and furthermore, you are not only ready for your soulmate, but also the positive transformation that a soulmate relationship will bring into your life. You are ready for the magic and miracles that this level of love can bring. You are ready to grow, become more of who you are, and give the great love that is in your heart to give. Finally...you are here, you are ready...and it is time.

I cannot wait to hear all of the magical stories about how your new soulmate relationship came into your life, at the perfect time and in the perfect way as a result of reading this book, following these steps and going through the program with me. I can't wait to see your smiling faces in the pictures you will post of your beautiful new life together and I couldn't be more excited to watch you 'knock it out of the park' in this area of your life too! I believe in you...I got your back...now go kick some ass girl!

Elizabeth Ward

Acknowledgements

First and foremost, I have to acknowledge my incredible soulmate, who because of how we met, not only inspired the process in this book, but believed in me so much and had my back so completely that this book and my program could come to be. I love you darlin', you will always be in my heart and I am so grateful that you came into my life so we could discover our shared passion for great food, funny animal vids, Maine coon cats, dreaming big dreams, travel, and nature photography...your generously sweet, smart-ass and strong energy was so perfect for me in every way at this time of my life.

To my soulmate clients, I consider it my own personal miracle whenever one of you "finds" me and walks into my program and into my heart. You have no idea what a joy and delight it is to work with you through this process as you find your own soulmate and to see your hope, joy and light multiply exponentially because of it. I am delighted and inspired every day that I get to serve you.

To my heart friends (you know who you are), thank you for seeing, believing in, and bringing out the best in me, especially when I couldn't. Your continued support and acceptance of my (often winding) path has meant the world to me.

Elizabeth Ward

About the Author

Elizabeth Ward has a master's degree in Psychology, is the author of the #1 Amazon book: Finding your Soulmate after 40 and the best-selling Positive Energy Oracle Card app, while simultaneously being a food lover of epic proportions and a part-time ninja warrior goddess. In her free time, she enjoys earning degrees that will never be put to practical use, binge watching sci-fi movies, and pondering the great mystery of what cats are really thinking.

Website: PositiveEnergyGal.teachable.com
Email: PositiveEnergyGal@gmail.com
Facebook: @PositiveEnergyGal
YouTube: Positive Energy Gal

My soulmate clients (you know who you are 'cuz you just got chills) can get more info about my programs at positiveenergygal.teachable.com.
I look forward to connecting and having fun with you!

About the Publisher

Positive Energy Publications is an Indie Publications Company empowering authors to get the positive messages in their heart...out into the world!
PositiveEnergyPublications.com

∞ ∞ ∞

More titles by **Positive Energy Publications***:*
Finding your Soulmate after 40: The Smart Woman's Guide
7 Simple Steps to Non-Toxic Gardening: A guide for the overwhelmed, eco-conscious, first-time gardener
#BrokenHeartedWisdom